THE BEST OF
MATT
2010

MATTHEW PRITCHETT

studied at St Martin's School of Art in London and first saw himself published in the *New Statesman* during one of its rare lapses from high seriousness. He has been the *Daily Telegraph*'s front-page pocket cartoonist since 1988. In 1995, 1996, 1999, 2005 and 2009 he was the winner of the Cartoon Arts Trust Award and in 1991, 2004 and 2006 he was 'What the Papers Say' Cartoonist of the Year. In 1996, 1998, 2000, 2008 and 2009 he was the *UK Press Gazette* Cartoonist of the Year and in 2002 he received an MBE.

Own your favourite Matt cartoons. Browse the full range of Matt cartoons and buy online at www.telegraph.co.uk/photographs or call 020 7931 2076.

The Daily Telegraph

THE BEST OF

MATT

2010

An Orion paperback

First published in Great Britain in 2010 by
Orion Books
A division of the Orion Publishing Group Ltd
Orion House
5 Upper St Martin's Lane
London WC2H 9EA

An Hachette UK company

10 9 8 7 6 5 4 3 2

A CIP catalogue record for this book
is available from the British Library

ISBN 978 1 4091 0375 2

Printed in the UK by CPI William Clowes, Beccles NR34 7TL

The Orion Publishing Group's policy is to use papers that
are natural, renewable and recyclable products and
made from wood grown in sustainable forests. The logging
and manufacturing processes are expected to conform to
the environmental regulations of the country of origin.

www.orionbooks.co.uk

THE BEST OF
MATT
2010

'If I was wearing exploding underpants I'd set them off right now'

'I've made a string of promises I can't possibly keep'

'*Sit down! The rules don't allow you to make a cup of tea while this is on*'

First ever TV debates

'It cuts Nick Clegg out of
the leaders' debate'

'Too much eye contact
makes me feel queasy'

The Election

'Don't worry, I'm tweeting that you won'

'While you're talking I'm drawing the audience reaction worm'

Instant reaction

'Vote Labour or Gordon Brown will pay you a visit'

Gordon's gaffes

The Election

Nick can do no wrong

Tactical voting

The Election

'You know we close
at 10pm, don't you?'

'Oh, all right then, take
me to Nick Clegg'

Uncertainty

'My horse won't win,
but it may hold the
balance of power'

'Is there something for
removing a Prime Minister
from Downing Street?'

Brown clings on

'The problem with the Lib Dems is you never know where they've been'

Lib Dems deal with Labour

'David Cameron can't give you a cabinet job just because you voted Lib Dem'

Deal sealed with Tories

Clegg and Cameron

'When I understand this
I'm going to be furious'

'I'll say one thing for George
Osborne, he's certainly
simplified the tax system'

'I'm afraid there's no money left. Good luck'

'That's how much the emergency budget is going to hurt!'

'Aaaaahh! I can see the national debt in 3D'

'I was doing austerity before it was fashionable'

The Economy

'I was wishing everyone a
Happy New Year, but
I've had to revise
that downwards'

New taxes

'I've been panic buying
taramasalata'

'A EURO! I say, old chap,
aren't they endangered?'

European problems

'I know I'm rich and unpopular, but I can't remember if I'm a banker or an MP'

The banks

'I've warned you about
excessive risk taking'

'I didn't realise numbers
went this small'

'We're breaking up your gigantic bonus into three enormous ones'

The banks

'Could you hide £1.5bn inside a Christmas pudding?'

'I missed you soooo much'

'If bonuses keep on rising, by 2050 parts of London could be under 4ft of money'

'My husband's too mean to turn up the heating, he just grits the hallway'

'That aftershave you gave me has de-iced the path brilliantly'

Snow

'We must stop seeing each other. My husband is becoming suspicious'

'I think the dog wants to go out'

Snow

'Chips are £1.
If you want salt on
them it's an extra £50'

'The village shop has
sold out of everything'

Shortages

'They knew the exams were coming, why weren't they better prepared?'

'Paying cash bonuses is a little awkward, so here's a bag of grit'

Post strike

'The brazier is going out.
Get some more letters'

'So there's a chance you won't be getting so many home shopping catalogues?'

'I'm posting it to my grandson. He's eight at the moment'

Post strike

'I'm posting a cheque to the expenses inquiry. Make sure it's not delivered'

'We have this huge backlog of "Sorry You Were Out" cards to deliver'

Duncan's gaffe

'Our bell tower certainly puts those upwardly mobile ducks in their place'

More excess

MPs' expenses

'And is your daddy an MP?'

'The gardener has decided
to stand against you at
the next election'

'This is your local MP...'

'Let's pretend I'm a brave army officer and you're an MP fiddling his expenses'

British Airways

'We have to cross the
picket line to get to the loo'

'Is this lunch or an
escalation of your
industrial action?'

'Sorry, I keep crashing...
I'm really a pilot'

'Could it be in a
suitcase somewhere?'

'I've just read the Lisbon Treaty. We're going to have to move that lot to Brussels'

Lisbon Treaty

Europe gets a president

Class War

'Turn off that chandelier!
Don't you know there's
a class war on?'

'Give up these crazy dreams
son. We don't know anyone
in the jellied eel business'

'I find the braking problems have stopped me worrying about my carbon footprint'

'Recall?'

BBC

'Swingeing cuts were announced today…'

Dear BBC,
On hearing what you have been paying your executives, I swore loudly in front of my children before the 9pm watershed.

Climate Talks

'I'm dreaming of a white Christmas, just like the ones I used to know...'

'My husband's a real sceptic. He doesn't even believe that Denmark exists'

'I hear you have some really strong, top grade, 100 watt light bulbs'

Wimbledon

'The match is over.
You can come out now'

'Play is suspended.
The roof is melting'

Another stressful Murray match

'Last time he barbecued something they grounded all flights over the UK'

Dubai

'I know what to do with our
debt mountain – let's
have it gold plated'

'A new shed! That's the sort
of vulgar excess that got
Dubai in such trouble'

'Let's say that jumper is
my wife and the other
one is your girlfriend'

'Since when did you
understand the
offside rule? Are you
seeing a footballer?'

Affairs . . .

'Excuse my husband. He was an early, unsuccessful attempt at artificial life'

'You've all been invited to
a photo shoot with
President Sarkozy'

'This will just reinforce
the stereotype image
of the French'

'Congratulations, son, you've turned from a boy into a suspected paedophile'

'You sneak into children's bedrooms looking for their teeth?'

CRB

'No, we're not going to waterboard any of the witnesses'

'I'm dreading the official inquiry into all this'

Tiger Woods

'You've got to avoid
the fire hydrant and
Tiger Wood's car'

'I couldn't get
any mistletoe'

'If this is about sex, we already know'

'I don't really mind, but I can't put their paintings on the fridge any more'

Brown's temper

'He threw his
moral compass at me'

'My homework is to colour
in EVERY country that
Gordon Brown has upset'

'At some time in the next
few weeks you're going
to see daddy cry...'

'If you missed it, England's World Cup exit will be repeated in four years' time'

England meet Germany . . .

'We're developing a potato that can open the batting for England'

'Mr Brown has apologised to dinosaurs for the asteroid that wiped them out'

And finally . . .

'I used to be an economic forecaster but it was all so hit and miss'

'If the wedding is next June, you should wear a flat screen TV showing the World Cup'

'Sorry, it was the only card I could get'

And finally . . .

'Ooh, today we've got a picture of a dead polar bear'

'I have decided to forgo a bonus this year'

And finally . . .

And finally . . .

'That's enough about the deficit, now has anyone got any fishing stories?'

'Great news! It was only really, really awful'

'And who's been using this address on her school admission form?'

'How embarrassing, I'm wearing the wrong tie. This is the one for Islam4UK'

And finally . . .

'I know it's cruel, but
he's been specially bred to
help with the crossword'

'If I don't have it on a
chain round my neck
I forget where I left it'

'The Government has raised the OMG level to the maximum'

'Gentlemen, we've developed a missile that ignores legal advice'

And finally . . .

'Is that the new iPad?'

'When the UK population
is 70 million we'll look
back at this as the
golden age of motoring'

'I ran so fast for the bus
that the driver demanded a
gender verification test'

'It seems that, before a
day's hunting, they'd listen
to Wake Up to Wogan'

And finally . . .

'How can I discover Anglo Saxon gold if I can't find my damn metal detector?'

And finally . . .

'Typical! The estate agent
didn't mention the
avocado bathroom suite'

'Red sky in the morning,
slow broadband warning'

And finally . . .

'The wind turbine provides all the power for the CCTV camera'

'I'm writing a blog. How many 'p's in disappointing?'

'Is that one of those no-frills airlines?'

Man's jet wing flight

'When people say it's back to the 70s, they're talking about industrial relations'

And finally . . .

'Can I speak to Nick Clegg about repealing certain laws? It's quite urgent...'

'These are Churchill's teeth, or as we call them, The Few'

CAPT. OATES AND THE RURAL BROADBAND

'I am just going online. I may be some time'

And finally . . .

And finally . . .

'You're not going out
dressed like that,
young lady'

'I have only £17.50 left.
Do you have any ailments
in that price range?'

'It's the most violent
computer game you can buy'

'We've been married for
34 years. It was a sham
wedding that went wrong'

And finally . . .

'You're under arrest. Go to the police station and let yourself into a cell'

END OF THE SPECIAL RELATIONSHIP?

'I think we should both start seeing other countries'

'Your pension will be fine
as long as you don't do
anything rash like retire'

'That isn't one of the laws
Nick Clegg is scrapping'

A Q&A with MATT

'It's pretty good,
but you're no Adolf Hitler'

Q **What's your favourite Matt cartoon?**

A Two paintings by Adolf Hitler were auctioned a couple of years ago. They were much better than everyone expected and I did this cartoon. For some reason it always makes me laugh.

Q **Is there any public figure or subject you wouldn't draw about and why?**

A I was about to say I never do jokes about people dying, but actually I have done some cartoons when a well-known celebrity has died. I try to make the cartoons a sort of tribute and a couple of times their friends and family have asked if the cartoon can be used at the funeral service.

Q **Have you ever regretted one of your cartoons?**

A With any jokes there's always a danger you'll upset someone. I did a lot of cartoons on the expenses scandal which I expect the MPs didn't find very funny, but none of them complained and a couple actually told me they'd enjoyed them.

Q **How did you get into drawing cartoons?**

A I went to art school and did a degree in graphic design. After I left I couldn't decide what to do. I knew I liked drawing, but I couldn't work out how it was going to feed and clothe me. I decided if I turned a drawing into a joke I might have more chance of getting it published. I'd never drawn a cartoon in my life, but I sent some off to magazines and after a very long time one got into the *New Statesman* and after that I never wanted to do anything else.

Q **Tell us about the process – how you come up with the idea, drawing, editing, final selection etc.**

A Lots of cartoonists work from home, but I need to be in an office with deadlines, post-it-notes, excitement, coffee machines, teamwork and gossip.

I start with a huge sheet of paper and along the top I write every subject in the news that I could do a joke on. I then try to fill the sheet with ideas. In the middle of the afternoon I quickly sketch my favourite six on an A4 piece of paper. Sometimes I find I only have five jokes that are good enough to

show the editor and I need to think
of one more to fill up the sheet;
that's always the one that gets
picked for the front page. The
others go in the bin. A topical joke
has the lifespan of a mayfly.

Then I start drawing. Sometimes
it goes well, but on other days it
just doesn't look right and I find
myself walking round the office
saying things like, 'Does that turkey
look like it's worried about
monetary union?'

One other thing I've noticed, if
you sneak up on a cartoonist while
they're drawing, they are always
pulling the expression they're
trying to draw.

Q Are there ever any slow news days
when you find it difficult to come
up with cartoon ideas?

A A quiet news day is a nightmare.

Q In the aftermath of 9/11 and
Princess Diana's death, the Matt
cartoon was sidelined. Why? And
do you think that was the right
decision?

A I just can't do serious cartoons and
I'd only make a national tragedy
worse if I tried.

Q It's rumoured that the married couple that regularly appears in your cartoons is based on real-life people who are unaware they are cartoon celebrities – care to elaborate?

A They were originally based on a real couple, but I think my wife and I are turning into them.

Q Would you ever make the transition into animation?

A When I was at art school we were told that for a second of animation you need to do more than ten drawings. That was when I lost interest.

Q You've been doing this for over 20 years – do you have any unfulfilled career ambitions?

A One of the things I like about working for a daily paper is I'm so busy with the next day's cartoon there isn't time for worrying about unfulfilled ambitions.